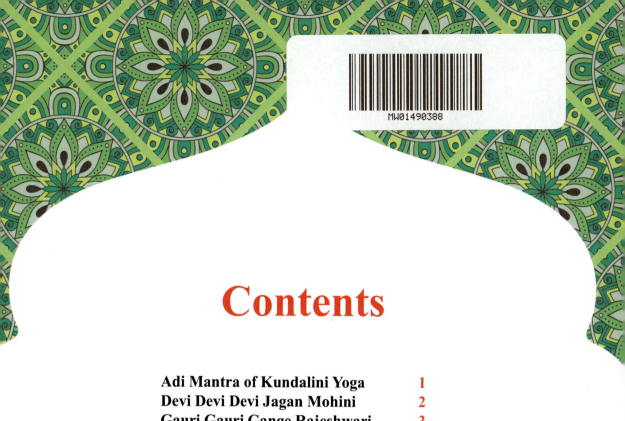

Contents

HOW TO HOLD AND PLAY YOUR KALIMBA

- Hold the kalimba with your your thumb on the keys and your other fingers on the side.
- Using your nails to strike the keys will minimize finger pain and make the sound more crisp.
- Use your middle finger to cover the hole on the back to create a WAH sound.
- Train your thumb to move easily between all the keys on each side.
- Tune with a mallet.

STANDARD 10-NOTE KALIMBA IN C SCALE

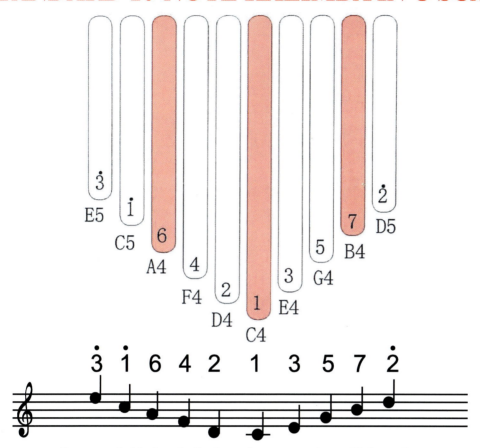

On most 8-10-tine kalimbas, the center tine will be a C note.

STANDARD 17-NOTE KALIMBA IN C SCALE

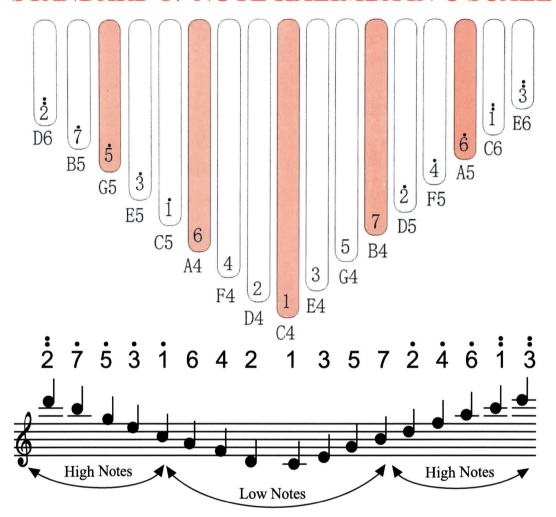

The low notes are usually in the center of a kalimba. The notes become higher as you move away from the center. The order of the notes alternate from right to left, going outward as you move up the scale. Taking "Do Re Mi Fa So La Ti Do", "Do" is on the right side, and then you will find "Re" on the left.

Also, the modern kalimba usually has enlarged letters representing the name of the notes. Often under the enlarged letter (or above the numbers), you can find one or two dots. These dots indicate the octave. Most kalimbas usually involve fourth, fifth and sixth octaves, and therefore can produce a high sound.

The central (the fourth normally octave) has no dots under the letters, the second (in reality fifth) is represented by one dot, and the third (sixth) has 2 dots under the letters. We also put one or two dots above the numbers in the sheet music if they use an octave other than the main kalimba octave.

Follow the numbers... and begin to play! This book might include only numbers and it will be enough to begin to play, but we decided to add classic note symbols to help teach them and show musical notation.

Attention: Songs have been transposed for a DIATONIC range. Some melodies might be changed and simplified.

Our sheet music is universal and suitable for 8-17 note kalimbas.

INDIAN MANTRAS ON KALIMBA

The kalimba is an African musical instrument that has a rather meditative quality since each sound can be observed separately. Although mantras are not typically played on the kalimba, you can have a unique spiritual experience nonetheless.

Mantras use the energy of sacred sound to bring benefit to the human body and psyche. The creation of this balance of energy has been used for centuries to access and open the human heart and mind, and connect them to physical and spiritual powers.

All mantras collected in this book originate from Hinduism and if you love yoga, meditation or are interested in Indian culture, playing mantras will evoke a deep resonance in your heart.

Each song has a QR code. Follow the link and listen to the rhythm before beginning to play.

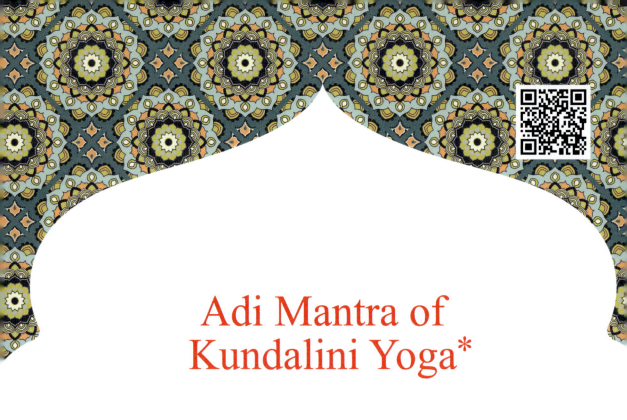

Adi Mantra of Kundalini Yoga*

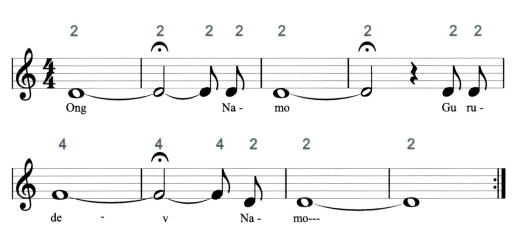

Ong   Na - mo   Gu ru -

de - v   Na - mo---

* Sikh Tradition

Devi Devi Devi Jagan Mohini

Gauri Gauri Gange Rajeshwari

Gayatri Mantra

Green Tara Mantra

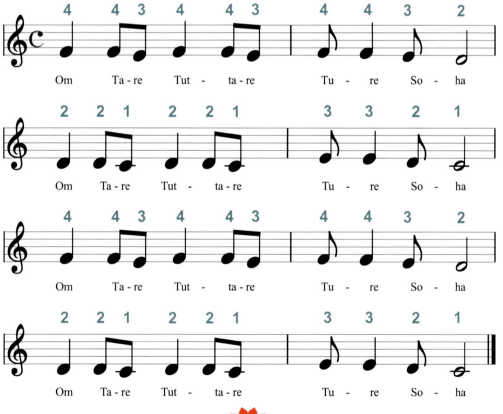

Hara Hara Mahadeva

Hare Krishna

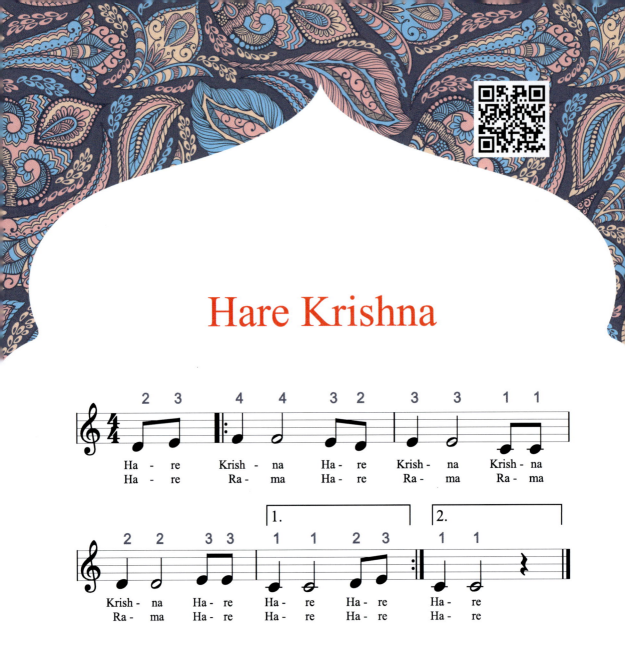

Jai Radha Madhav Kunjabihari

Jaya Ho Mata

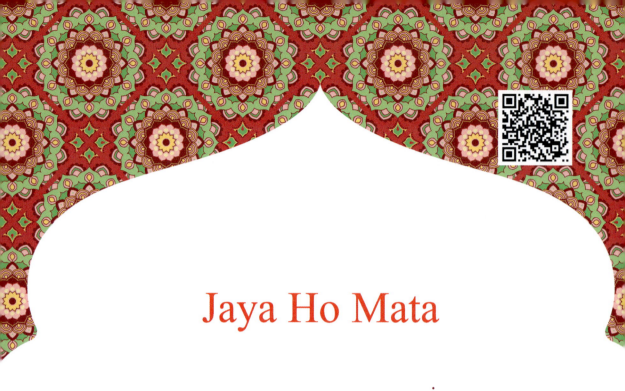

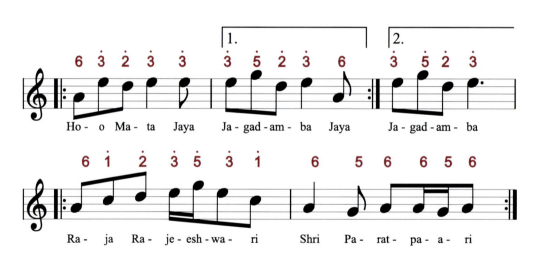

Kali Durgai Namo Namah

Lokah Samastah Sukhino Bhavantu

Maha Mrityunjaya Mantra

Namo Tassa Bhagavato (Vandana)*

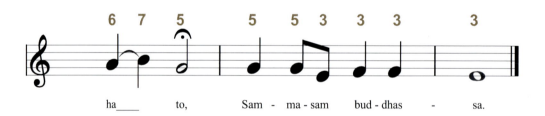

* Theravada Buddhist Tradition

Om Bhagavan

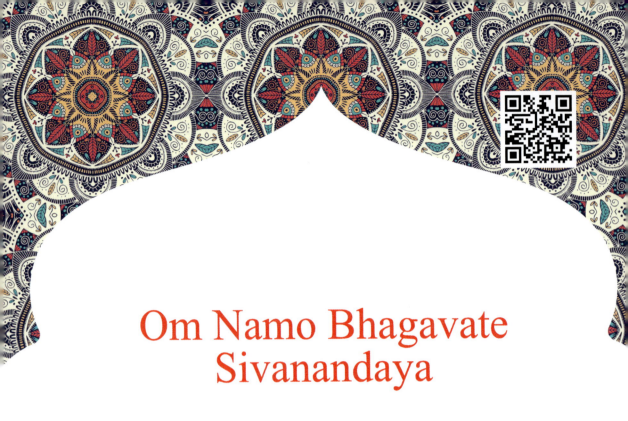

Om Namo Bhagavate Sivanandaya

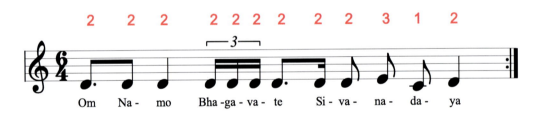

Om Shakti Om

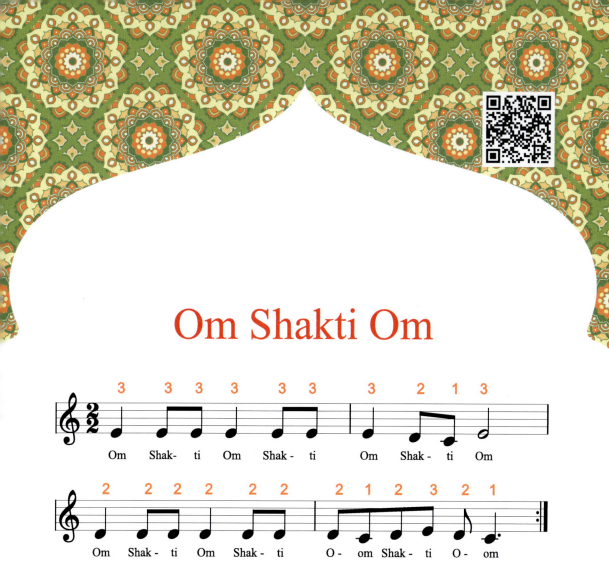

Shankara Karunakara

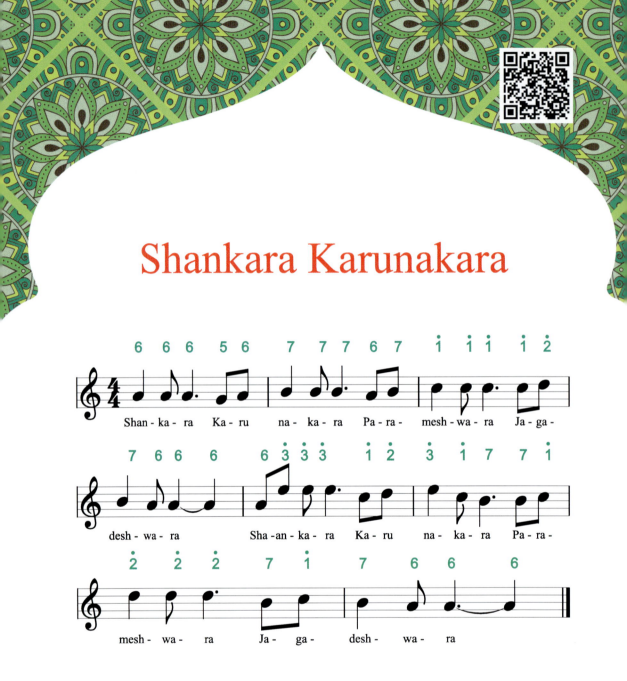

Shivananda Namah Om

Shivaya Parameshwaraya

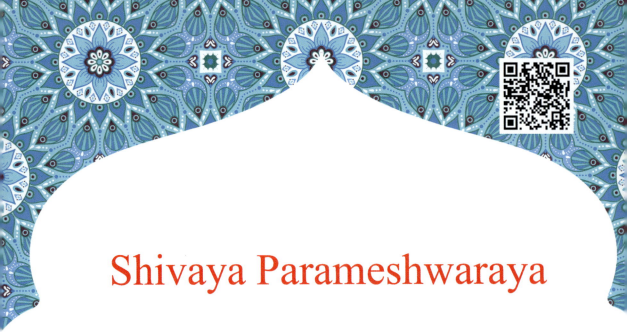

Siri Gayatry Mantra*
(Ra Ma Da Sa)

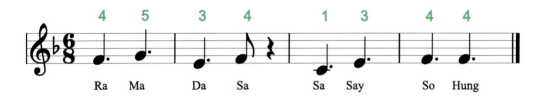

* Sikh Tradition

Made in the USA
Las Vegas, NV
27 December 2023

83583413R10017